bright spark
brilliant brain
cool kid
superstar
great work
amazing work

I Can Learn

Adding and Subtracting Skills

Written by David Kirkby

Illustrated by John Haslam

This book belongs to
....

EGMONT

Tips for happy home learning

Make learning fun by working at your child's pace and always giving tasks which s/he can do. Tasks that are too difficult will discourage her/him from trying again.

⭐

Give encouragement and praise and remember to award gold stars and sticker badges for effort as well as good work.

⭐

Always do too little rather than too much, and finish each session on a positive note.

⭐

Don't work when you or your child is tired or hungry.

⭐

Reinforce workbook activities and new ideas by making use of real objects around the home.

EGMONT
We bring stories to life

Copyright © 2005 Egmont Books Limited
All rights reserved.
Published in Great Britain by Egmont Books Limited,
239 Kensington High Street, London W8 6SA
www.egmont.co.uk

Printed in Italy.
ISBN 1 4052 1567 4
6 8 10 9 7

One more

⭐ 3

Count the spots on each card and write the number which is one more.

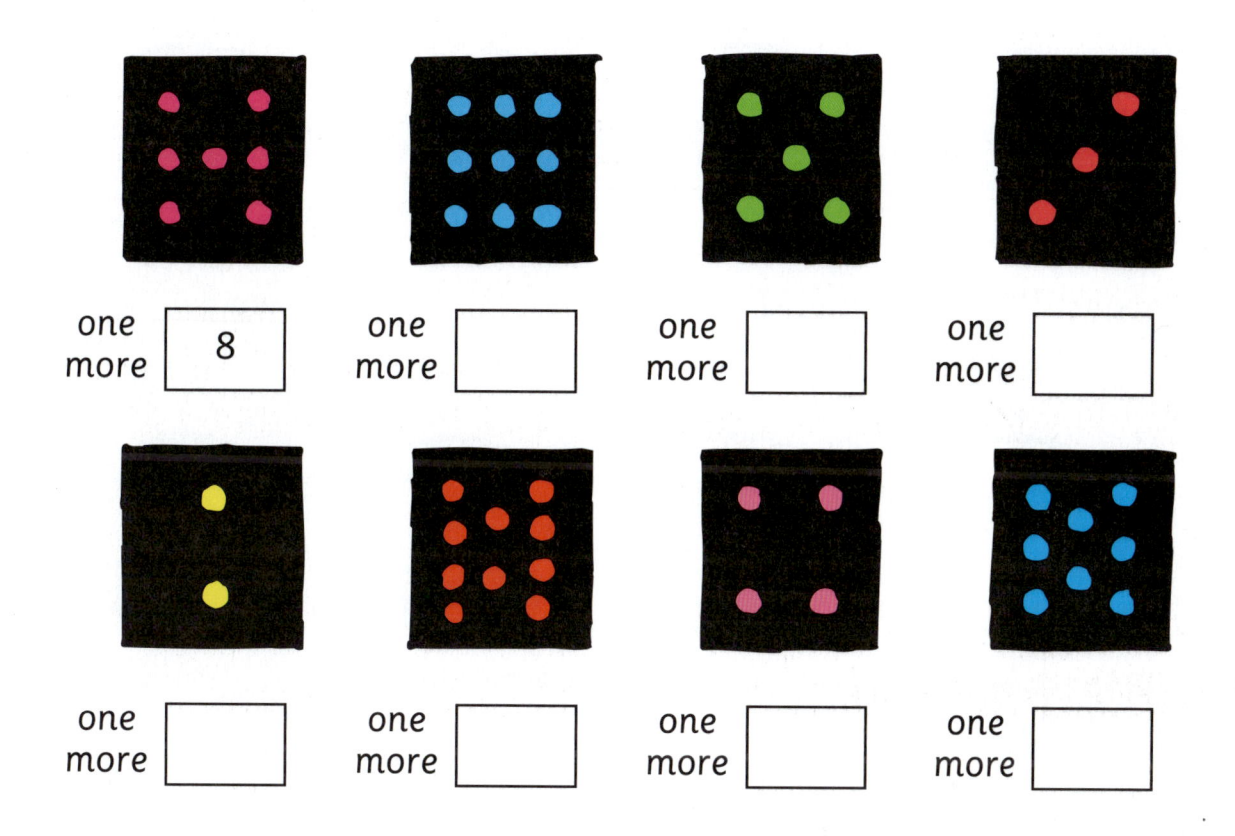

| one more | 8 | one more | | one more | | one more | |

| one more | | one more | | one more | | one more | |

Write one more than each number on the grid.

3	9	0	5
2	8	6	2
9	1	7	4
7	6	8	3

one more →

4	10		

Well done. Choose a sticker.

4 ★ Two more

Count the biscuits on each plate and write the number which is two more.

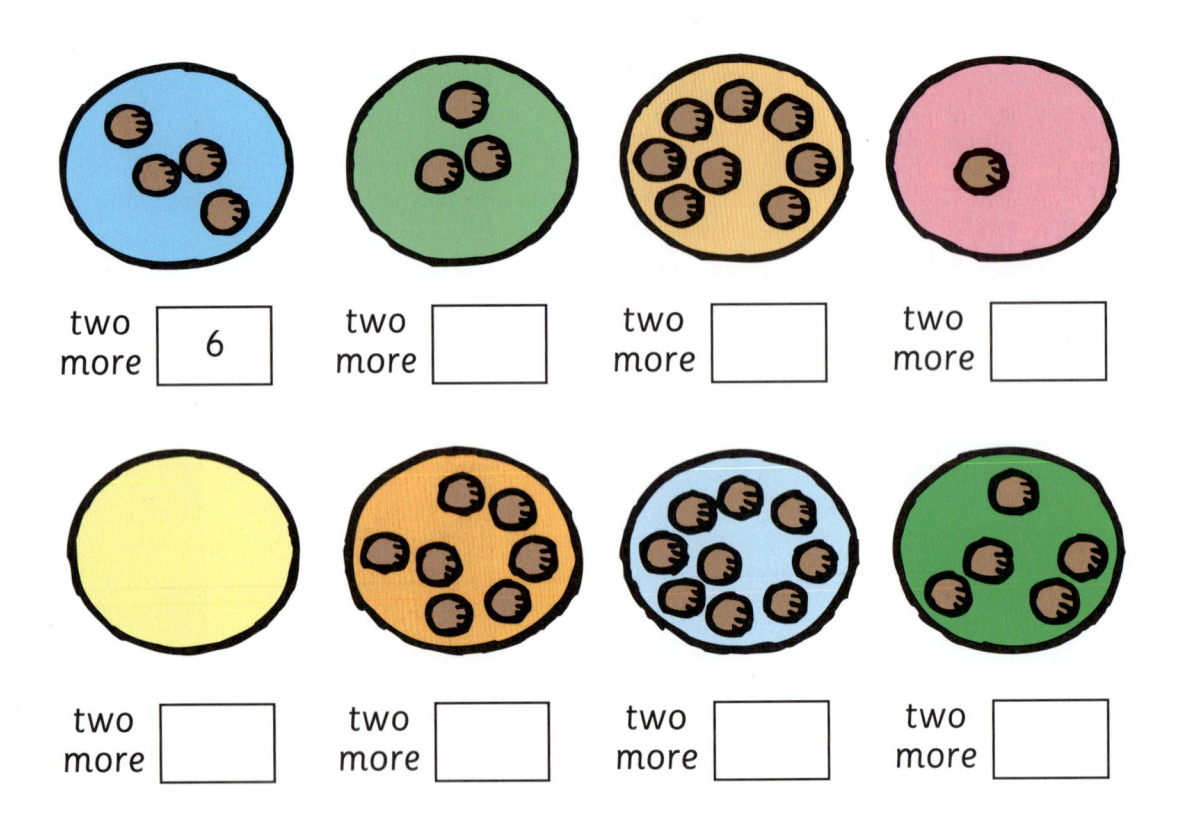

two more [6]   two more [ ]   two more [ ]   two more [ ]

two more [ ]   two more [ ]   two more [ ]   two more [ ]

Write two more than each number on the honeycomb.

2, 7, 5, 8, 9, 6, 4, 9, 1, 0, 7, 3, 6, 10, 5, 4 → two more → 4, 9

Draw two more busy bees.

Adding (up to 10) ⭐ 5

Draw all the cakes on the two small plates on the big plate, then write the addition.

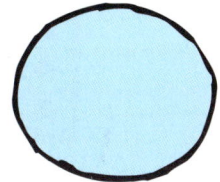

[3] add [2] = [5]   [ ] add [ ] = [ ]

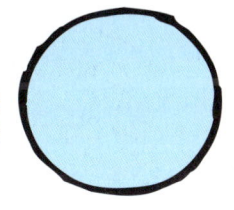

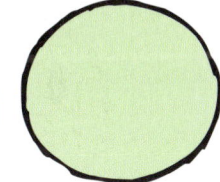

[ ] add [ ] = [ ]   [ ] add [ ] = [ ]

Count the circles and triangles in each set, then add them together.

(4) + △5 = [9]

◯ + △ = [ ]

◯ + △ = [ ]

Use your fingers to count if you get stuck.

Adding (up to 12)

Add the spots on each pair of dice.

6 + 3 = 9

☐ + ☐ = ☐

☐ + ☐ = ☐

☐ + ☐ = ☐

Add the spots on each pair of shapes.

4 + 2 = 6

☐ + ☐ = ☐

☐ + ☐ = ☐

☐ + ☐ = ☐

What a lot of spots!

Adding

Complete these additions.

1 + 2 = 3   3 + 4 = ☐   4 + 4 = ☐

5 + 3 = ☐   2 + 3 = ☐   8 + 1 = ☐

1 + 6 = ☐   6 + 2 = ☐   3 + 7 = ☐

Complete these number strips.

add 2

1	6	2	4	0	5	3	7
3	8						

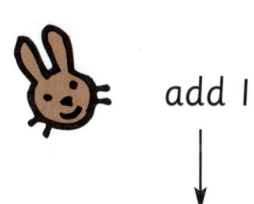

add 1

7	2	9	3	5	6	0	8

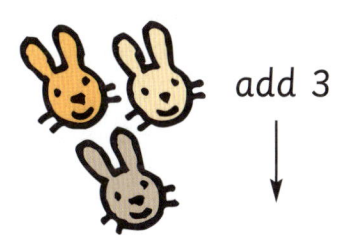

add 3

4	6	0	3	5	2	7	1

Well done, choose a sticker or star.

Making ten

8

These dominoes have a total of 10 spots each.
Draw in the missing spots on the blank sides.

These pairs of cards make ten.
Can you write in the missing numbers?

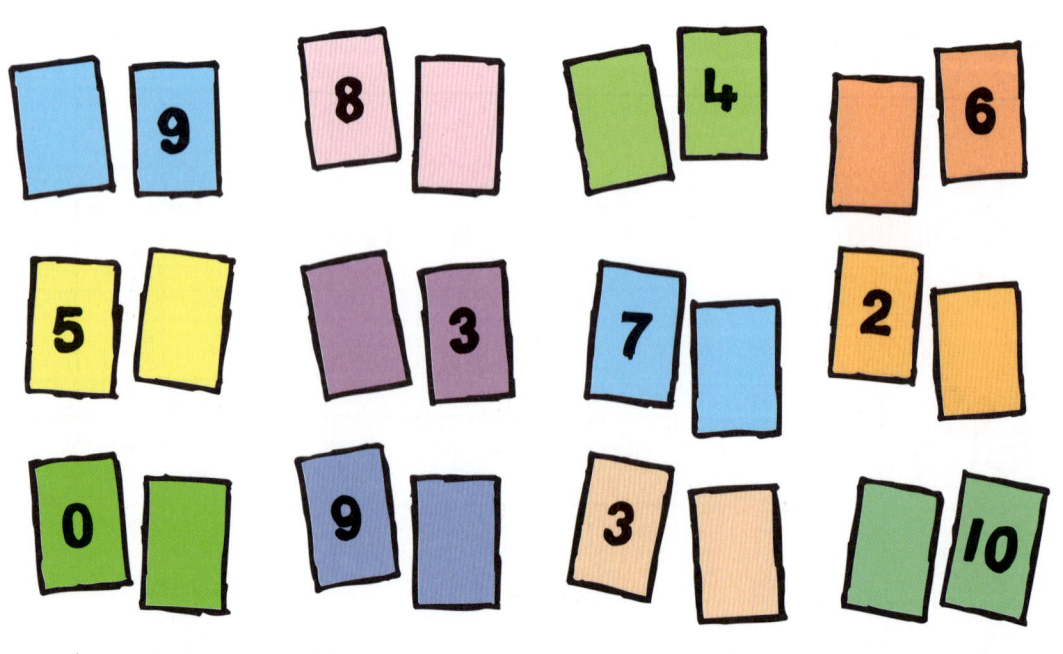

9

8

4

6

5

3

7

2

0

9

3

10

Perfect pairs. Great work!

Making 10

⭐ 9

Colour the balloons which add up to 10 in your favourite colour.

4 + 6   2 + 3   3 + 6   7 + 3
5 + 5   9 + 1   8 + 2   6 + 4

Write numbers on the right which make 10 with the numbers on the left.

4	1	6	9
3	7	0	5
2	5	8	7
10	6	4	3

make 10 →

6	9		

How many balloons did you colour?

10 One less

Count the spots on each card and write the number which is one less.

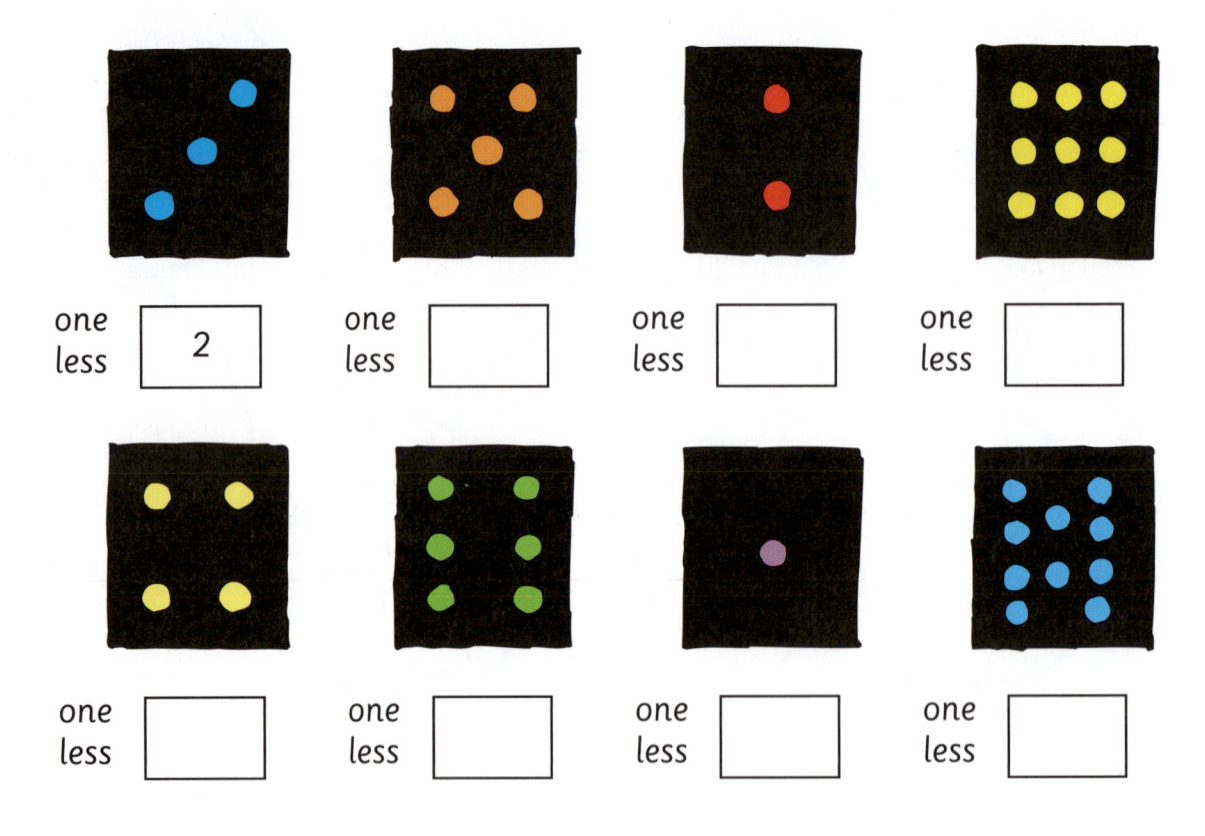

one less [2]   one less [ ]   one less [ ]   one less [ ]

one less [ ]   one less [ ]   one less [ ]   one less [ ]

Write one less than each number on the grid.

5	9	2	8
10	1	7	6
4	6	3	9
8	7	10	5

one less →

4	8		

Wonderful work, help yourself to a star.

Two less

Count the chocolates on each plate and write the number which is two less, the first is done for you.

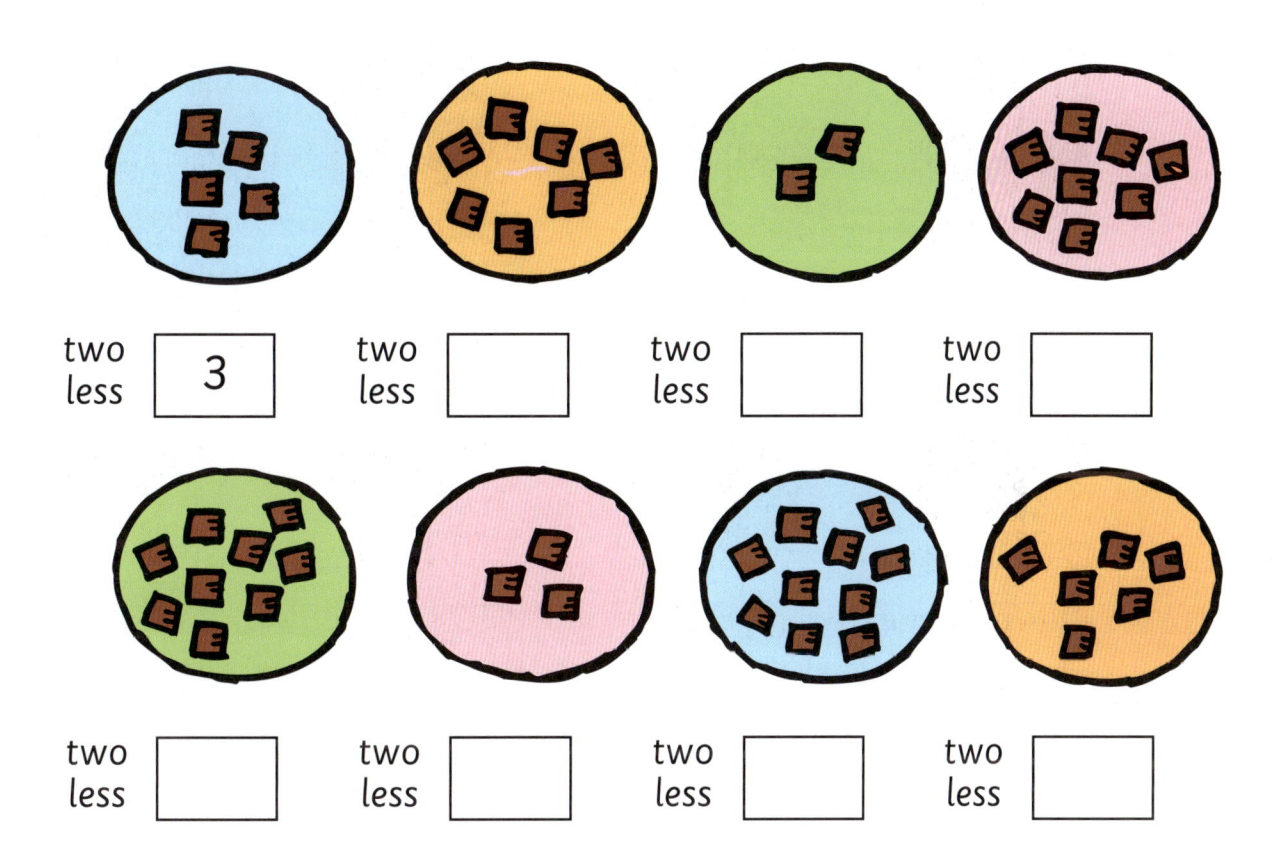

two less: 3
two less: ☐
two less: ☐
two less: ☐

two less: ☐
two less: ☐
two less: ☐
two less: ☐

Write two less than each number on the honeycomb.

4 8 9 3
11 6 5 10
7 9 2 7
8 4 6 5

two less →

2   6

Note for parents: Use real objects, such as buttons, pennies or sweets to help with taking away.

12 Taking away

Take three apples away from each bowl, then write in the numbers.

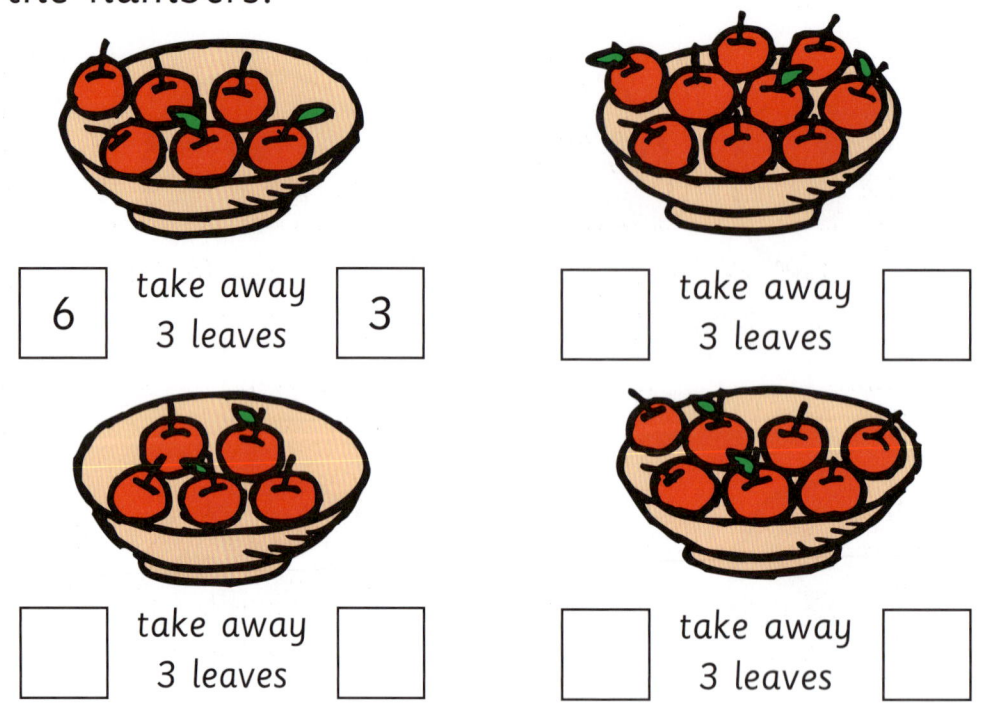

| 6 | take away 3 leaves | 3 |

| ☐ | take away 3 leaves | ☐ |

| ☐ | take away 3 leaves | ☐ |

| ☐ | take away 3 leaves | ☐ |

Take two away from each set of bananas.

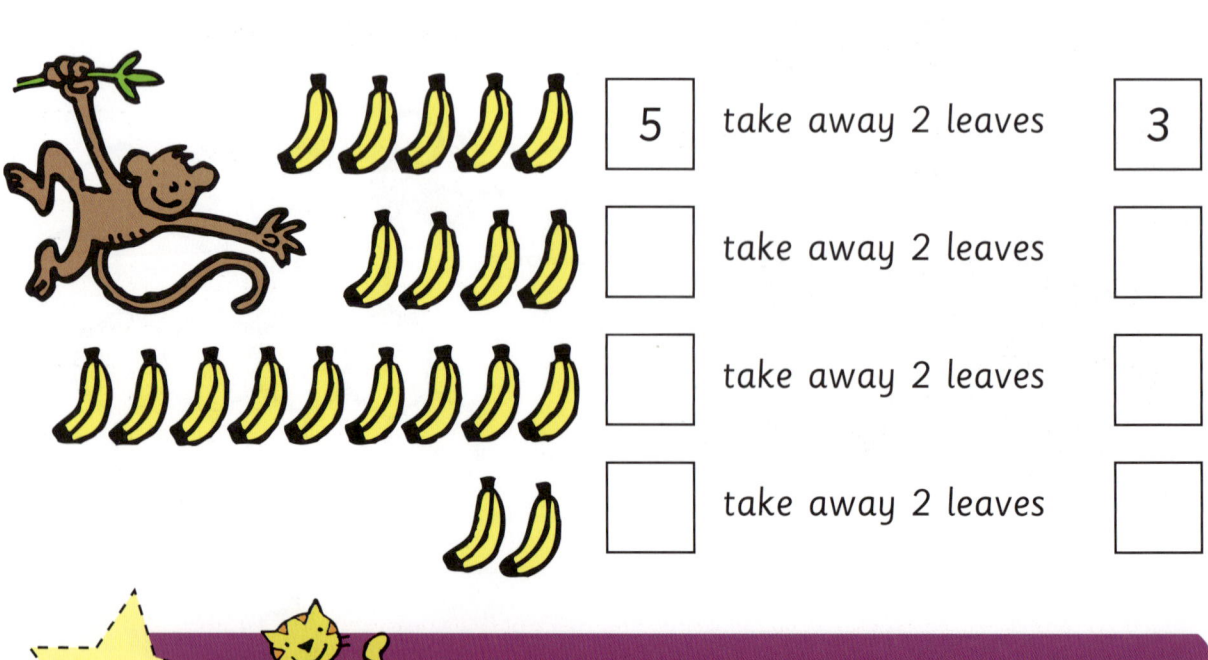

5	take away 2 leaves	3
☐	take away 2 leaves	☐
☐	take away 2 leaves	☐
☐	take away 2 leaves	☐

This is making me hungry!

Taking away

13

Take away spots from the cards.
Draw them.

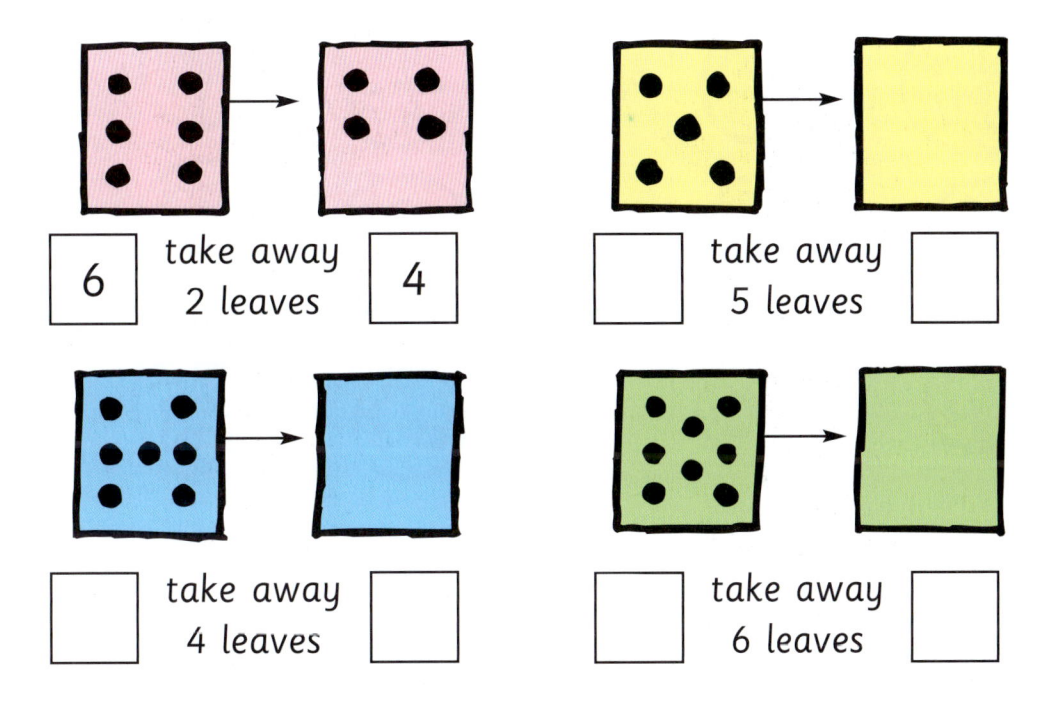

| 6 | take away 2 leaves | 4 |

| | take away 5 leaves | |

| | take away 4 leaves | |

| | take away 6 leaves | |

Cross out the shapes to take them away.

| 6 | take away 2 leaves | 4 |

| | take away 5 leaves | |

| | take away 1 leaves | |

| | take away 4 leaves | |

Excellent work!

Adding money

Write the total of these sets of coins.

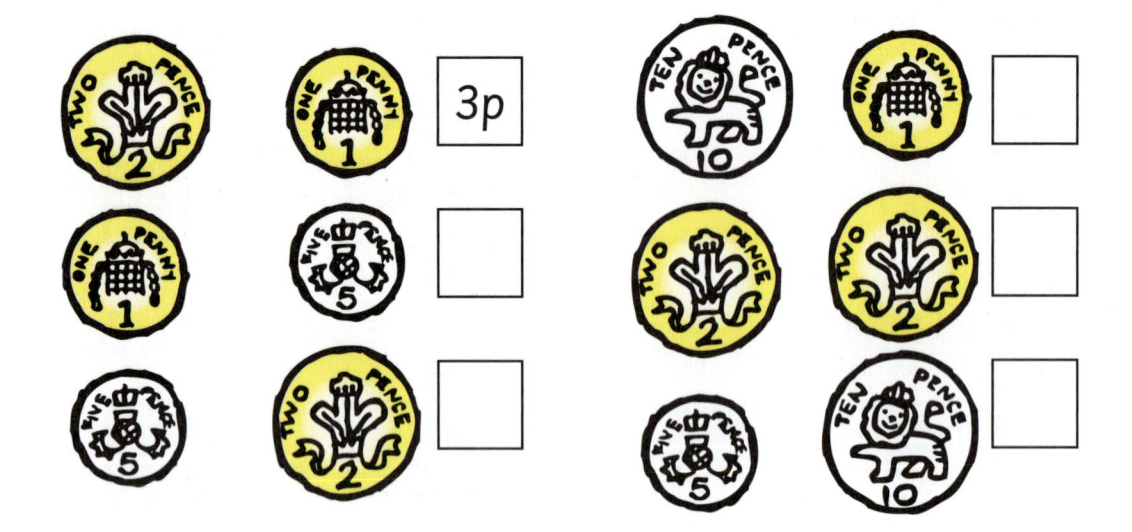

2p + 1p = 3p
10p + 1p = ☐

1p + 5p = ☐
2p + 2p = ☐

5p + 2p = ☐
5p + 10p = ☐

Sweets:

- Choc bar 6p
- Chewy 4p
- Lolly 3p
- Gobstopper 2p
- Sherbet 5p

Write down the price of:

a choc bar and a chewy. **10p**

a lolly and a sherbet. ☐

a gobstopper and a choc bar. ☐

two choc bars. ☐

three sherbets. ☐

a gobstopper and a chewy. ☐

Which sweets would you choose with 10p?

Equations

Draw the spots on the blank dice to make these totals.

5 + ☐ = 8   3 + ☐ = 7

4 + ☐ = 9   6 + ☐ = 10

4 + ☐ = 8   1 + ☐ = 7

Complete the additions by writing in the missing numbers.

1 + [3] = 4   7 + ☐ = 10

4 + ☐ = 8   2 + ☐ = 7

☐ + 5 = 11   ☐ + 7 = 9

☐ + 3 = 3   4 + ☐ = 10

How did you do?

16 Subtracting

Complete these subtractions.

4 − 1 = [3]   7 − 3 = [ ]   5 − 2 = [ ]

10 − 4 = [ ]   9 − 6 = [ ]   8 − 7 = [ ]

6 − 3 = [ ]   10 − 9 = [ ]   3 − 3 = [ ]

Finish filling in these number strips.

take away 2

3	5	8	2	9	7	4	6
1	3						

take away 4

5	8	10	6	9	4	11	7

take away 3

6	8	4	10	7	9	3	5

Super number work!

Equations

17

Complete these subtractions by writing in the missing numbers.

6 − [2] = 4   7 − [ ] = 2

8 − [ ] = 5   4 − [ ] = 1

[ ] − 5 = 0   [ ] − 2 = 7

[ ] − 8 = 1   8 − [ ] = 2

Write numbers on the grid by taking away three from the numbers on the left.

9	6	4	13
5	8	10	7
11	3	5	9
8	12	6	7

take away 3 →

6	3		

Note for parents: Make up some more subtraction equations for your child to solve.

18 Adding

Write down the scores for each pair on this target.

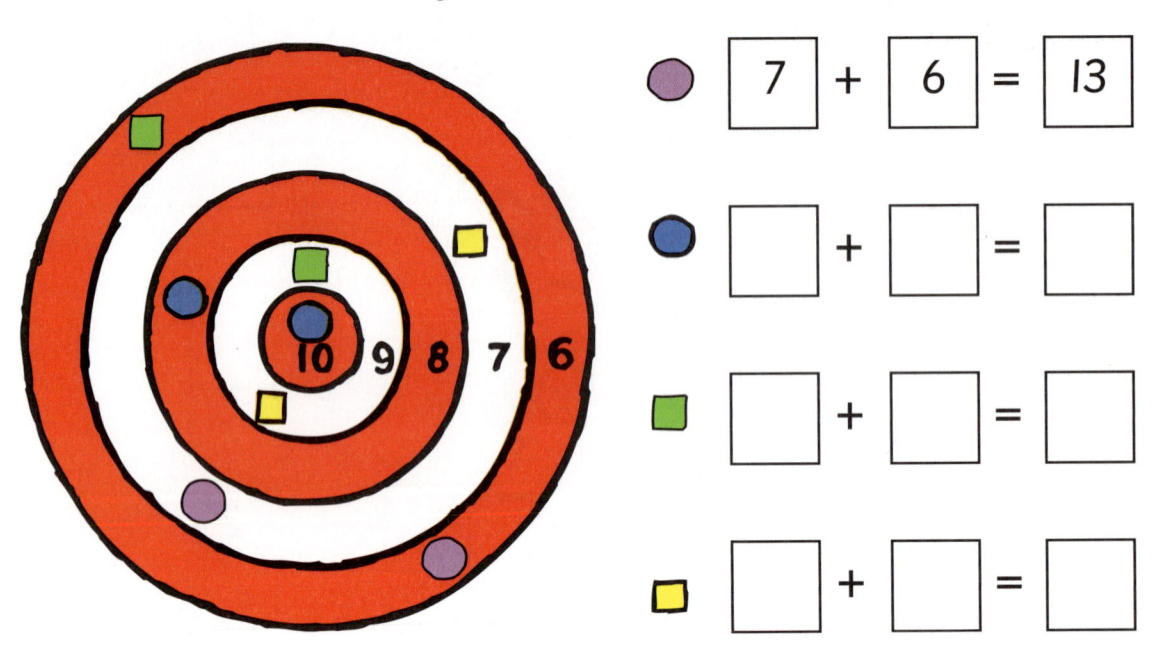

● 7 + 6 = 13

● ☐ + ☐ = ☐

■ ☐ + ☐ = ☐

■ ☐ + ☐ = ☐

Write down the total of the numbers on each pair of cards.

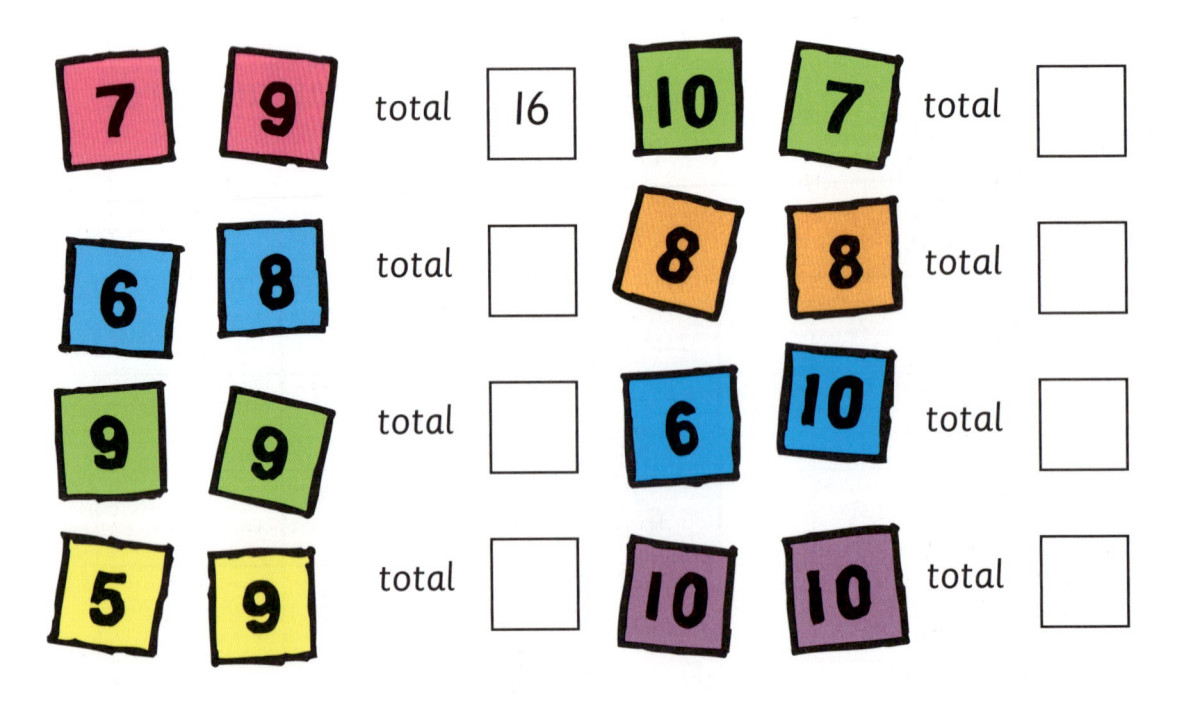

7 9   total 16
6 8   total ☐
9 9   total ☐
5 9   total ☐

10 7   total ☐
8   8   total ☐
6   10 total ☐
10 10 total ☐

Note for parents: This practises counting with numbers up to twenty. Again, you could use toy bricks, pencils or buttons.

Adding

Complete these additions.

5 + 8 = 13   6 + 12 = ☐   11 + 4 = ☐

7 + 9 = ☐   7 + 7 = ☐   8 + 8 = ☐

14 + 5 = ☐   6 + 4 = ☐   5 + 14 = ☐

Complete these number strips.

add 7

10	7	13	9	12	8	6	11
17	14						

add 4

14	9	16	11	12	7	13	15

add 6

12	7	8	11	13	9	14	10

You are brilliant at counting!

20 Differences

Write the differences between the heights of these pairs of towers.

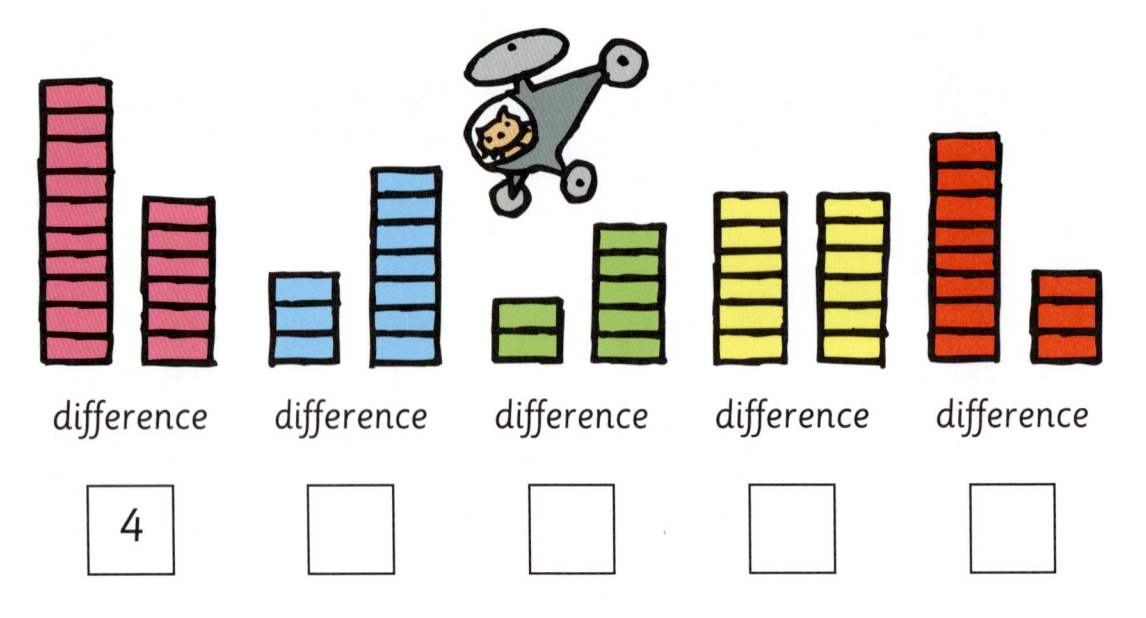

difference difference difference difference difference

| 4 | | | | |

Write the differences between the numbers on these pairs of cards.

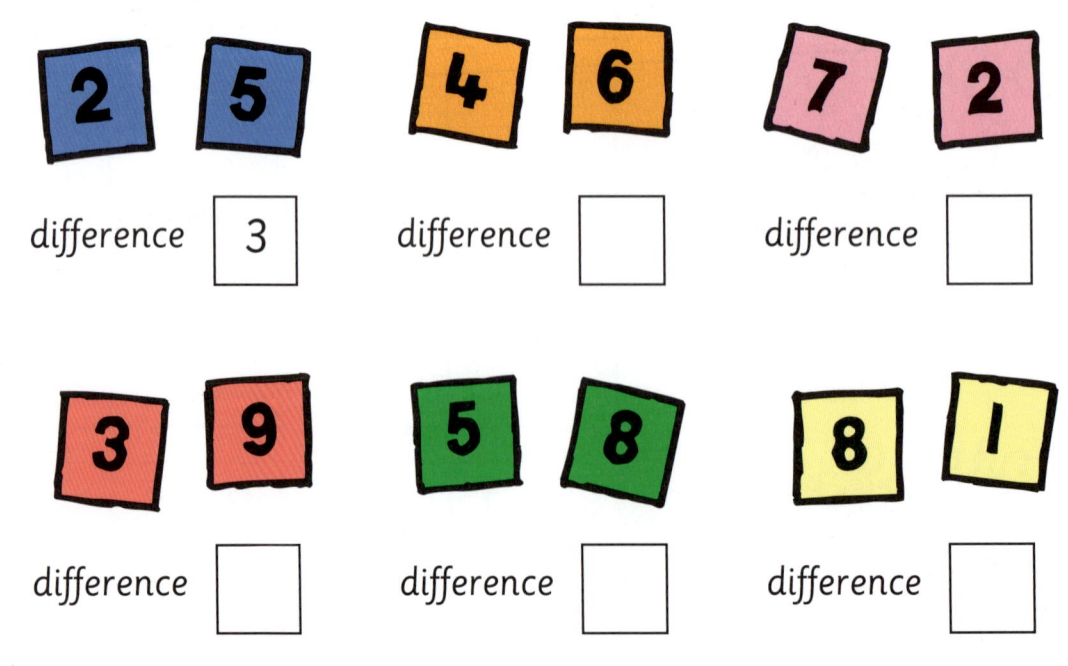

2 5   4 6   7 2

difference 3   difference ☐   difference ☐

3 9   5 8   8 1

difference ☐   difference ☐   difference ☐

You are doing very well.

Change from 10p

Write down the change from 10p for each of these.

- Pencil 6p — change: 4p
- Rubber 2p — change: ☐
- Pen 9p — change: ☐
- Ruler 7p — change: ☐

- Sticker 3p — change: ☐
- Labels 5p — change: ☐
- Notepad 10p — change: ☐
- Sharpener 8p — change: ☐

Walnut 2p   Chestnut 1p   Plum 4p   Pear 5p   Cherry 3p

Write down the change from 10p for:

1 walnut and 1 chestnut	change: 7p	3 chestnuts	change: ☐
2 cherries	change: ☐	2 plums and 1 chestnut	change: ☐
1 plum and 1 pear	change: ☐	2 walnuts and 1 cherry	change: ☐

Note for parents: Use real coins (1p, 2p, 5p) to help your child with this exercise.

22 Adding three numbers

Write down the totals of these dice.

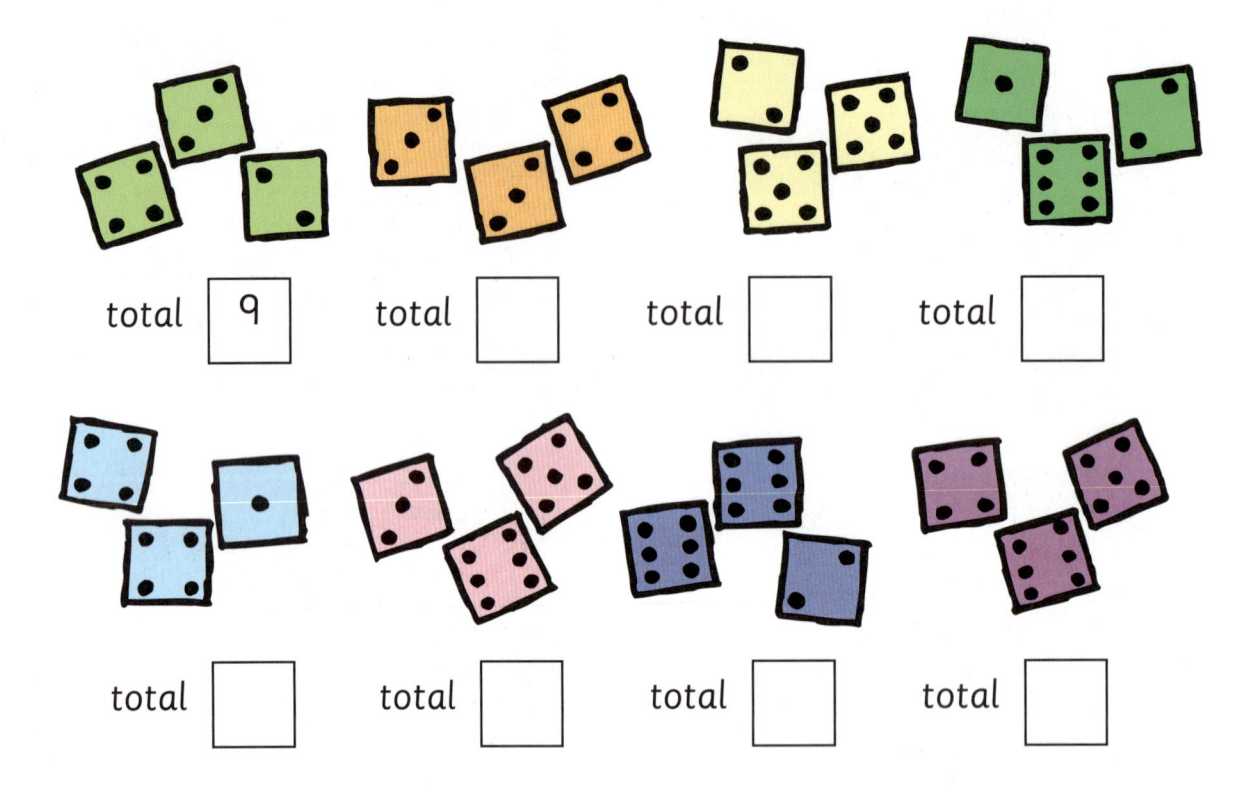

total [9]   total [ ]   total [ ]   total [ ]

total [ ]   total [ ]   total [ ]   total [ ]

Add the numbers in each row and each column of these grids.

7	4	2	→	13
1	6	8	→	
9	3	5	→	

2	8	1	→	
4	5	6	→	
7	3	9	→	

Note for parents: Make up a game to play with your child using three dice. The winner throws the highest score.

Adding three numbers

23

Write down the total of the three darts in each board.

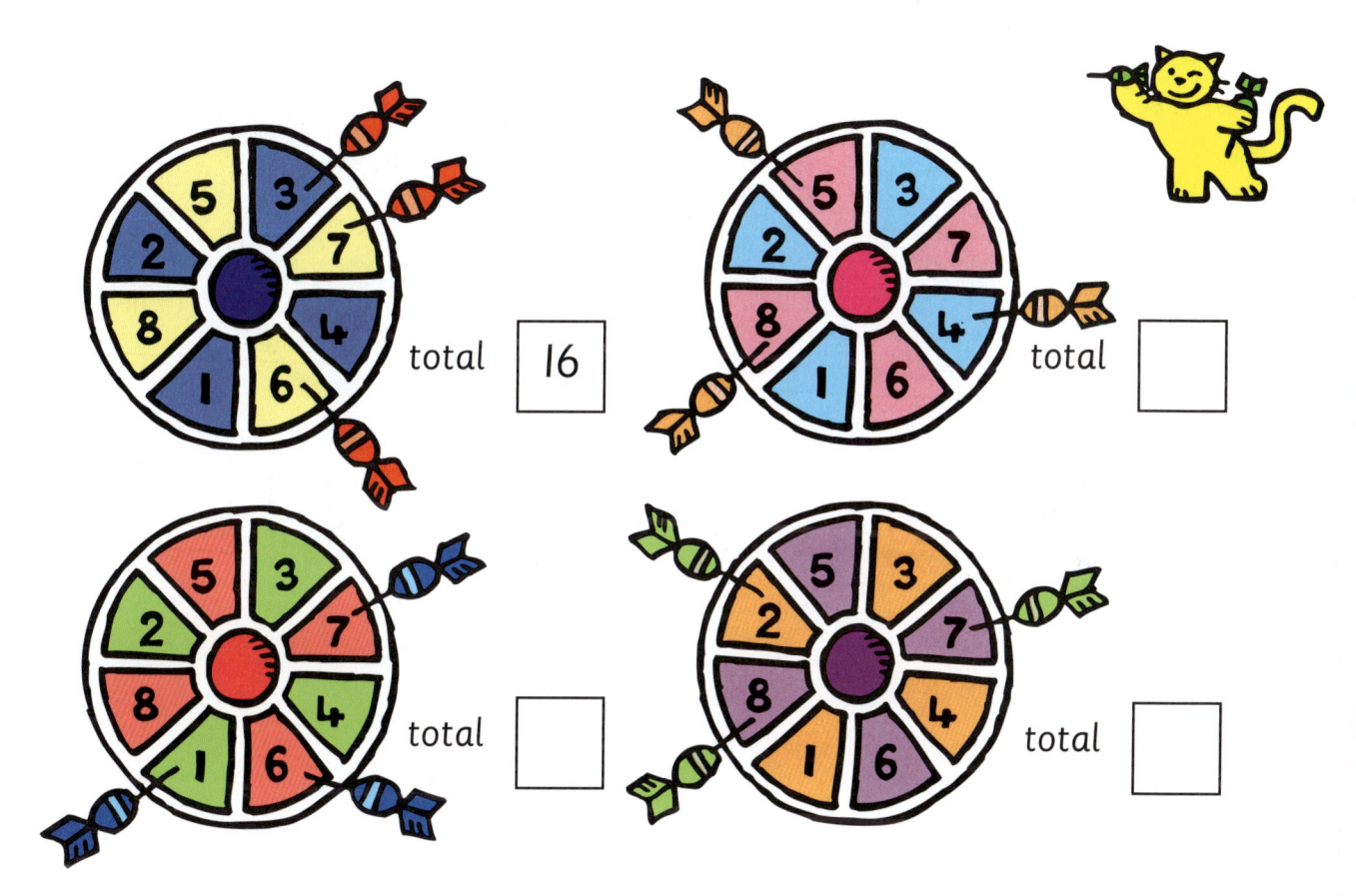

total 16

total ☐

total ☐

total ☐

Write down the scores for three shots at this target.

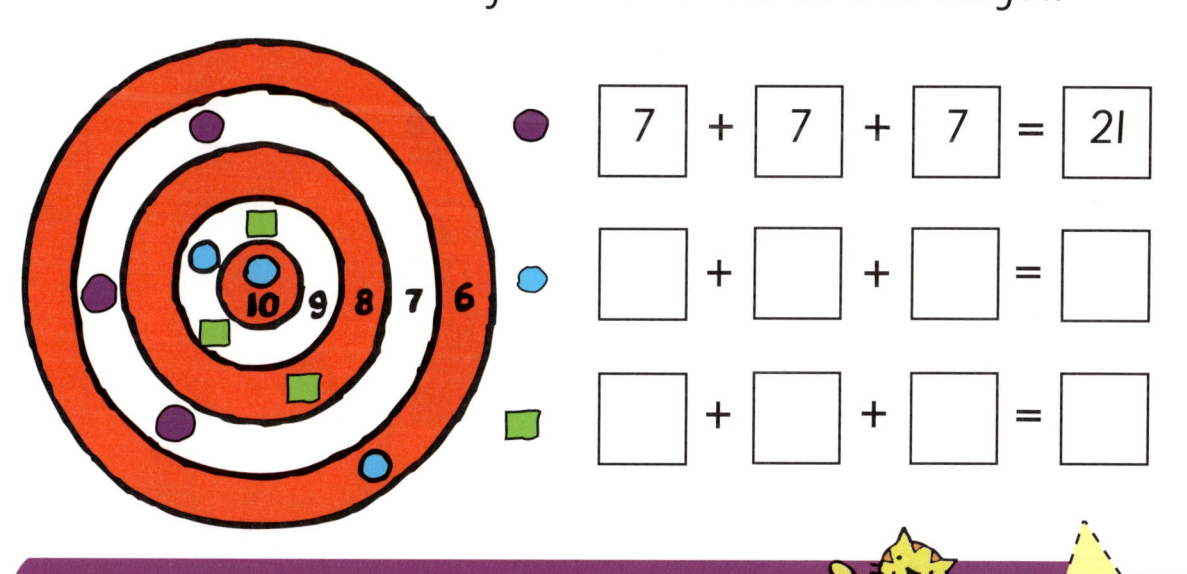

● 7 + 7 + 7 = 21

● ☐ + ☐ + ☐ = ☐

■ ☐ + ☐ + ☐ = ☐

Which shape scored the most points?

24 Adding money

Write the total of these sets of coins.

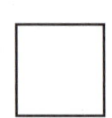

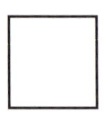

2p + 5p = **7p**

20p + 20p = ☐

1p + 10p = ☐

2p + 50p = ☐

5p + 20p = ☐

50p + 20p = ☐

Write down the price of:

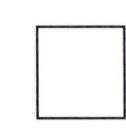

Prices:
- ONION 7p
- POTATO 8p
- LETTUCE 6p
- CUCUMBER 10p
- CABBAGE 9p

1 onion and 1 lettuce — **13p**

1 cabbage and 1 onion — ☐

1 cucumber and 1 potato — ☐

1 cucumber and 1 lettuce — ☐

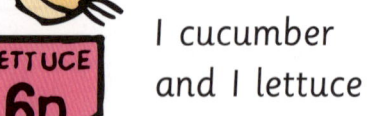

2 cabbages — ☐

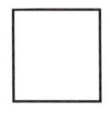

2 potatoes — ☐

1 potato and 1 lettuce — ☐

3 onions — ☐

Which vegetable is the most expensive?

Making twenty

These pairs of cards make 20.
Write in the missing numbers.

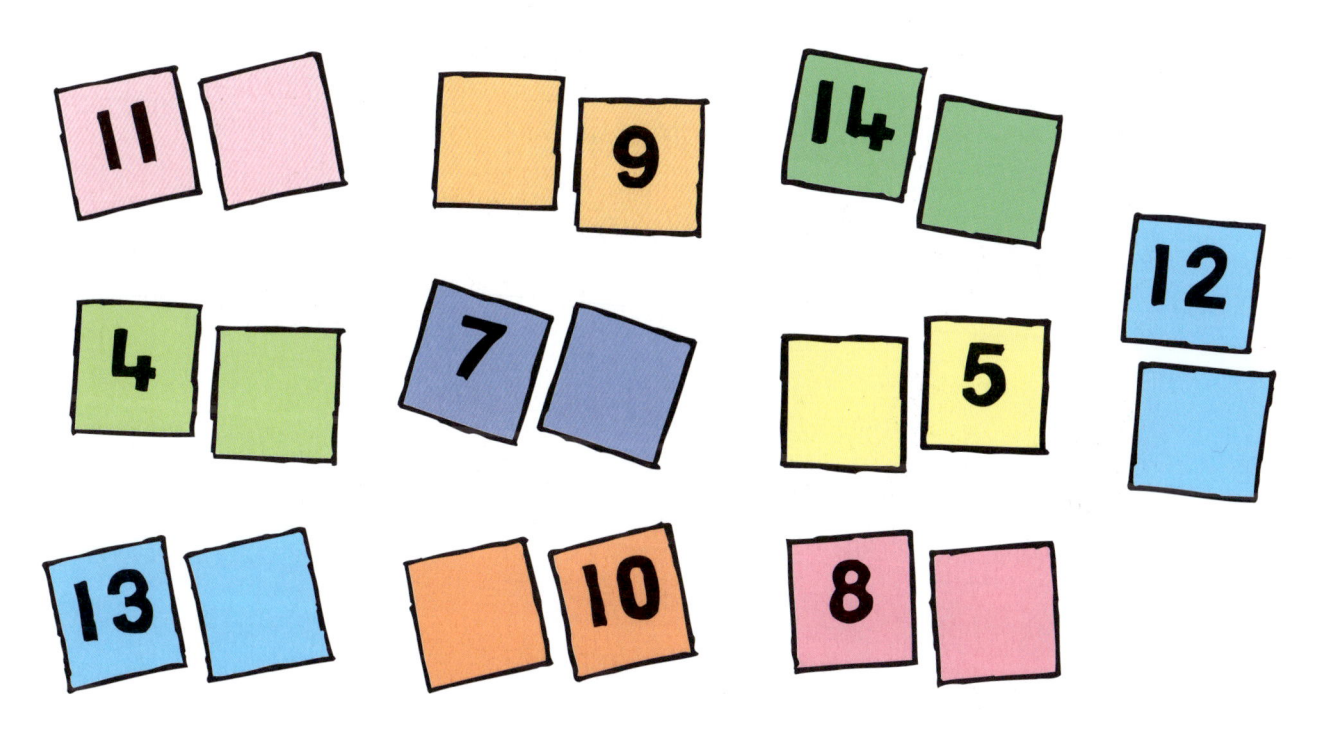

11 ☐	☐ 9	14 ☐
4 ☐	7 ☐	☐ 5	12 ☐
13 ☐	☐ 10	8 ☐

Write numbers on the right which make 20 with the numbers on the left.

6	11	14	7
10	3	16	5
15	12	9	18
8	17	4	13

make 20 →

14	9		

Note for parents: Make up some more addition equations for your child to solve.

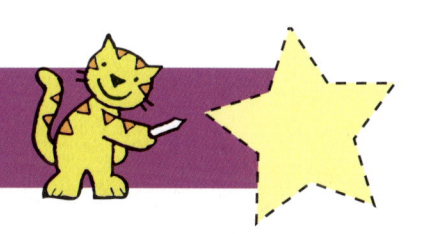

Subtracting

Complete these subtractions.

17 − 3 = [14]   16 − 14 = [ ]   19 − 13 = [ ]

20 − 11 = [ ]   14 − 9 = [ ]   12 − 9 = [ ]

13 − 8 = [ ]   15 − 4 = [ ]   18 − 5 = [ ]

Complete these number strips.

take away 4

13	10	19	14	20	15	9	17
9	6						

take away 7

11	16	8	18	13	17	9	15

take away 5

16	20	11	18	15	19	13	17

Terrific taking away!

Change from 20p

Write down the change from 20p for each of these.

Item	Price	Change
Magazine	15p	5p
Comic	18p	☐
Birthday Card	17p	☐
Note Pad	10p	☐
Newspaper	12p	☐
Sweets	7p	☐
Ice Cream	8p	☐
Lolly	6p	☐

Mint Bar 8p · Choco 6p · Kruncher 10p · Pluto Bar 9p · Nougat 7p

Write down the change from 20p for:

1 mint bar and 1 nougat — change 5p

2 crunchers — change ☐

2 pluto bars — change ☐

1 nougat and 1 choco — change ☐

1 choco and 1 pluto bar — change ☐

1 pluto bar and 1 mint bar — change ☐

Note for parents: On shopping trips, encourage your child to pay for things and check the change.

28 Adding

Complete these additions.

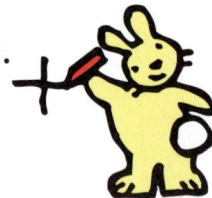

13 + 4 = [17]   46 + 1 = [ ]   37 + 2 = [ ]

22 + 5 = [ ]   53 + 6 = [ ]   12 + 7 = [ ]

35 + 3 = [ ]   42 + 4 = [ ]   24 + 5 = [ ]

Complete these number strips.

add 3

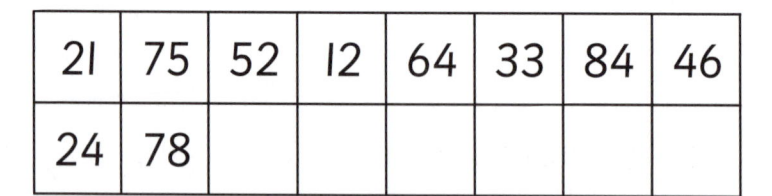

21	75	52	12	64	33	84	46
24	78						

add 5

11	54	93	60	24	43	72	31

add 2

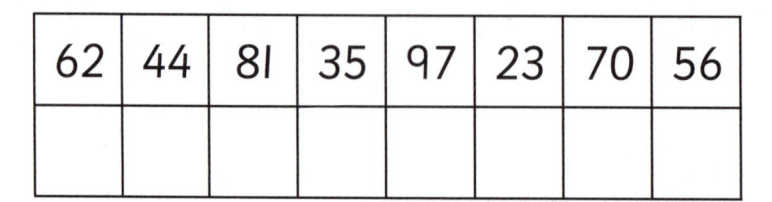

62	44	81	35	97	23	70	56

Time to choose another star or sticker.

Adding

⭐ 29

Can you add all these sets of cubes?

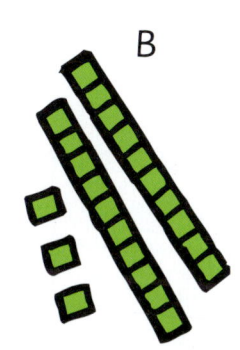

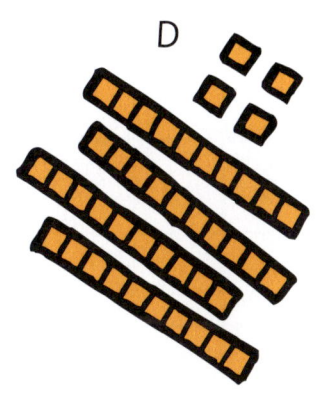

A   B   C   D

A and C

[32] + [13] = [45]

B and C

[ ] + [ ] = [ ]

C and D

[ ] + [ ] = [ ]

D and A

[ ] + [ ] = [ ]

Add the numbers on these pairs of cards.

22 62 31 24 37
32 27 14 64 21

[54] [ ] [ ] [ ] [ ]

Which cards add up to the highest number?

30 Adding (up to 20)

Complete these addition tables.

+	10	11	12	13
4	14			
5			17	
6				
7				

+	6	3	5	4
10				
12				
14				
11				

Add the numbers for each pair of shapes.

Triangle = 10, Diamond = 7, Circle = 8, Rectangle = 6, Pentagon = 9

Triangle + Diamond = 17

Rectangle + Triangle = ☐

Pentagon + Circle = ☐

Circle + Circle = ☐

Triangle + Circle = ☐

Rectangle + Pentagon = ☐

That was easy peasy!

Adding

Write numbers in each block of the pyramids. The number in each block is the total of the two numbers below it.

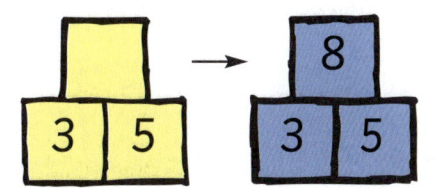

Complete these:

- 6 / 2, 4
- _ / 7, 6
- _ / 5, 8
- _ / 3, 7
- _ / 9, 9

Now these:

- 8 / 5, 3 / 3, 2, 1
- _ / _, _ / 4, 1, 2
- _ / _, _ / 3, 2, 5
- _ / _, _ / 2, 4, 6

And these:

- 20 / 9, 11 / 4, 5, 6 / 1, 3, 2, 4
- _ / _, _ / _, _, _ / 2, 1, 4, 5
- _ / _, _ / _, _, _ / 6, 2, 3, 4

Note for parents: For extra practise, you could draw some more number pyramids on a sheet of paper.

Equations

Write the missing numbers on these cards.

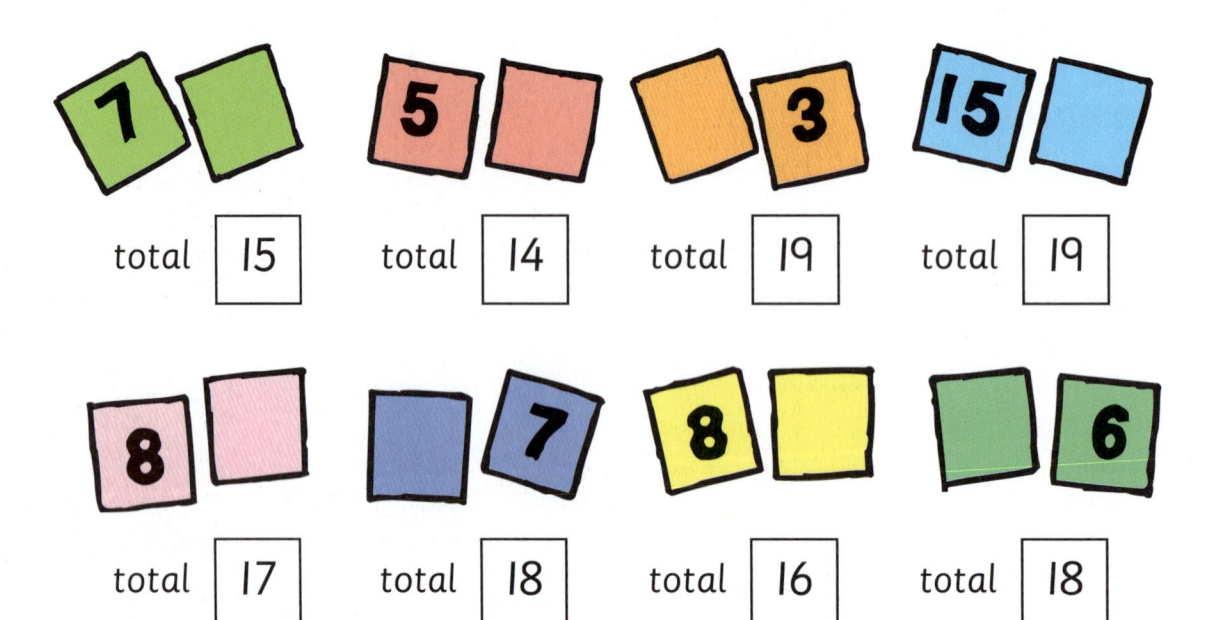

7 ☐	5 ☐	☐ 3	15 ☐
total 15	total 14	total 19	total 19

8 ☐	☐ 7	8 ☐	☐ 6
total 17	total 18	total 16	total 18

Complete these additions and subtractions by writing in the missing numbers.

$4 + \boxed{7} = 11$ $15 + \boxed{} = 19$

$\boxed{} + 12 = 20$ $\boxed{} + 7 = 16$

$20 - \boxed{} = 17$ $15 - \boxed{} = 6$

$\boxed{} - 11 = 7$ $\boxed{} - 8 = 5$

Super work. Choose a big gold star!